It's Not Catching

Bumps & Bruises

Angela Royston

www.heinemann.co.uk/library
Visit our website to find out more information about **Heinemann Library** books.

To order:
 Phone 44 (0) 1865 888066
 Send a fax to 44 (0) 1865 314091
 Visit the Heinemann Bookshop at www.heinemann.co.uk/library to browse our catalogue and order online.

First published in Great Britain by Heinemann Library, Halley Court, Jordan Hill, Oxford OX2 8EJ, part of Harcourt Education.
Heinemann is a registered trademark of Harcourt Education Ltd.

Editorial: Sarah Eason and Kathy Peltan
Design: Dave Oakley, Arnos Design
Picture Research: Helen Reilly, Arnos Design
Artwork: Tower Designs UK Ltd
Production: Edward Moore

Originated by Dot Gradations Ltd
Printed and bound in Hong Kong and China by South China Printing Company

The paper used to print this book comes from sustainable sources.

ISBN 0 431 02149 X
08 07 06 05 04
10 9 8 7 6 5 4 3 2 1

British Library Cataloguing in Publication Data
Royston, Angela
Bumps and bruises. – (It's not catching)
613.2

A full catalogue record for this book is available from the British Library.

Acknowledgements
The publishers would like to thank the following for permission to reproduce photographs:
Getty Imagebank p. **29**; Getty Images/Stone/Nick Dolding p. **11**; Last Resort p. **21**; Mark Harwell Stone p. **6**; Masterfile/Rommel p. **26**; Phillip James Photography p. **20**; Powerstock p. **26**; SPL p. **17**; SPL/Dr P Marazzi pp. **4**, **18**; SPL/Oscar Burriel p. **13**; Taxi/Carl Schneider p. **7**; Taxi/Steven Simpson p. **9**; The Image Bank/Ben & Esther Mitchell p. **8**; Trevor Clifford pp. **5**, **10**, **15**, **19**, **22**, **23**, **24**, **27**, **28**, **25**.

Cover photograph reproduced with permission of Trevor Clifford.

The publishers would like to thank David Wright for his assistance in the preparation of this book.

Every effort has been made to contact copyright holders of any material reproduced in this book. Any omissions will be rectified in subsequent printings if notice is given to the publishers.

Contents

Words written in bold, **like this**, are explained
in the Glossary.

What are bumps and bruises?

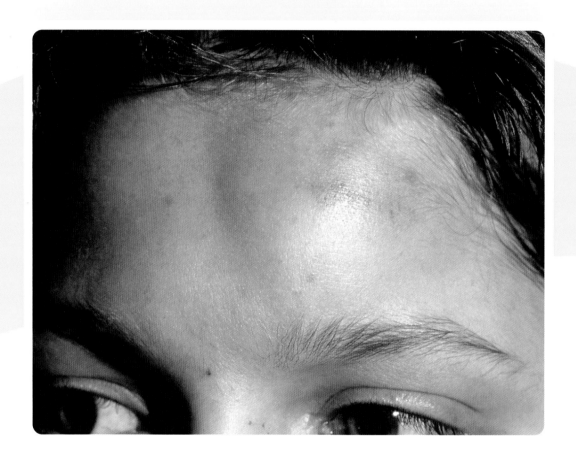

When your skin gets a hard knock or bang, it may form a **bump** or a **bruise**. A bump is a hard lump that forms over the part that was banged.

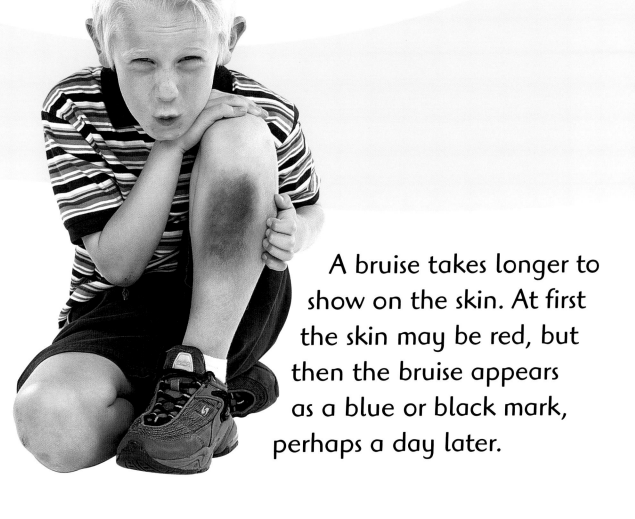

A bruise takes longer to show on the skin. At first the skin may be red, but then the bruise appears as a blue or black mark, perhaps a day later.

Who gets bumps and bruises?

Anyone who falls heavily, or who is hit hard, is likely to get a **bump** or a **bruise**. Children and older people are most likely to fall.

People who play sports, such as football, cricket or baseball, are also likely to get bruises from time to time. You cannot catch a bump or bruise from someone else.

Falls

You are likely to fall when you trip over something, or when you lose your **balance**. It is hard to keep your balance when you learn to skateboard!

The faster you are going when you fall,
the more likely you are to **injure** yourself.
The harder the knock, the bigger the **bump**
or **bruise**.

Bangs

You bang yourself when you bump
into something, or when something hits
your body. You might bump into a table,
for example. Most bangs and bumps
are **accidental**.

10

But sometimes one person hits another person on purpose. People should not hit each other hard because they can hurt each other. Boxers use gloves to soften their punches.

Trapped fingers

Children sometimes get their fingers trapped in a drawer or a door. Do not hold the edge of a door or the door frame. Your fingers will get trapped if someone shuts it.

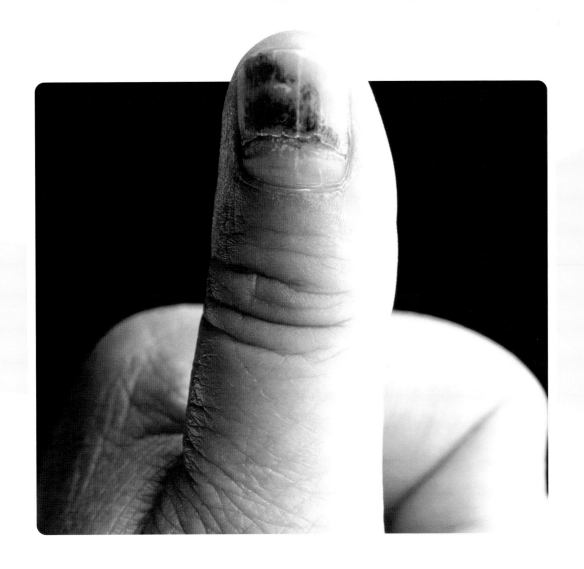

If your fingers have been trapped, your fingernails may become **bruised** and black. If the base of the nail is damaged, the whole nail may even fall off.

Inside a bump

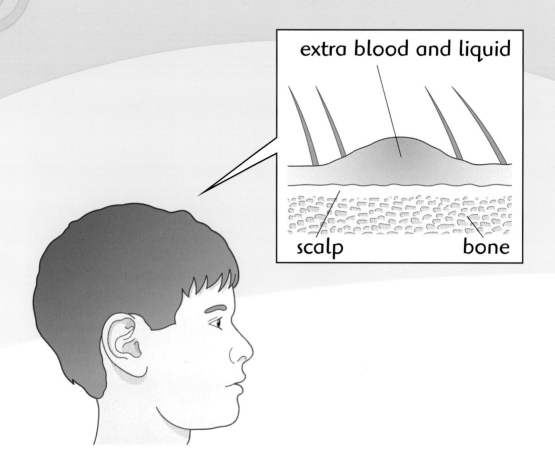

extra blood and liquid

scalp   bone

A **bump** is made of **swollen** flesh, blood and other liquid made by the body. A bump feels hard, and hurts when you touch it.

Your body forms a bump to protect the **injury** while it heals. The extra blood helps the injury to heal. As the injury heals, the bump goes down.

Inside a bruise

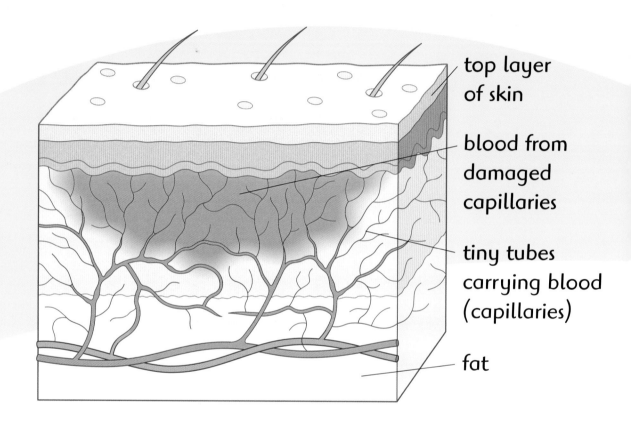

top layer of skin

blood from damaged capillaries

tiny tubes carrying blood (capillaries)

fat

Your skin is fed by tiny tubes of blood, called capillaries. Each tube is as narrow as a single hair. When your skin is banged, some of the tubes burst. This makes a **bruise**.

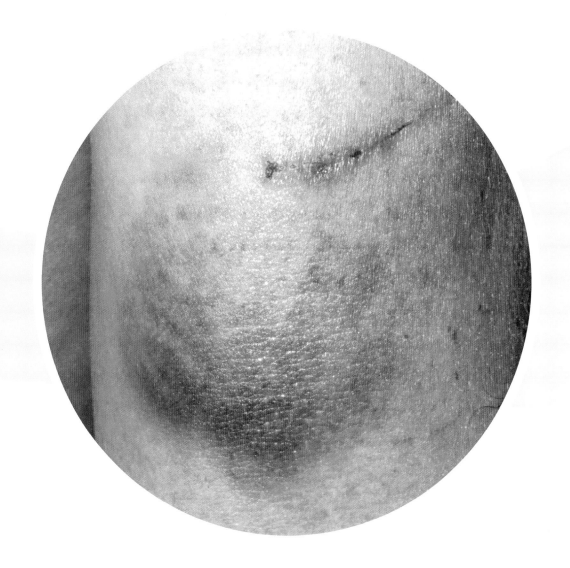

The blood leaks into the **flesh** around the
bang. As the spilled blood dies, it turns black.
You see it as a bruise through your skin.

Bangs on the head

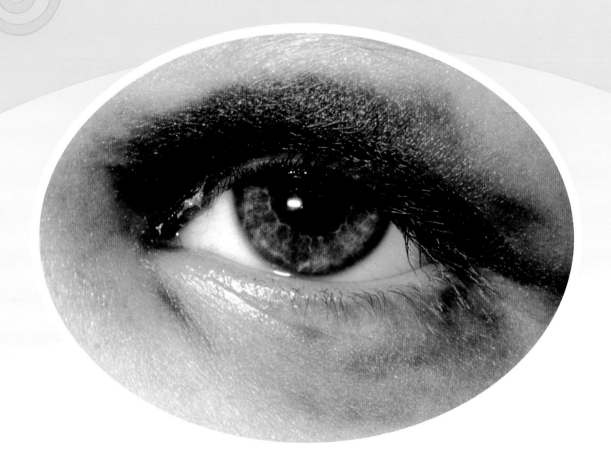

Your head and face easily become **bruised**.
You do not have much fat or muscle between
the bones and the skin to cushion any
bumps and bangs.

Head **injuries** can be dangerous because
your head includes your **brain**, eyes, ears,
nose and mouth. A hard bang on the head
can cause serious injury.

Serious head injuries

If your head is hit very hard, you may knock your **brain**. This is called **concussion** and makes you feel confused. You may become **unconscious** for a time.

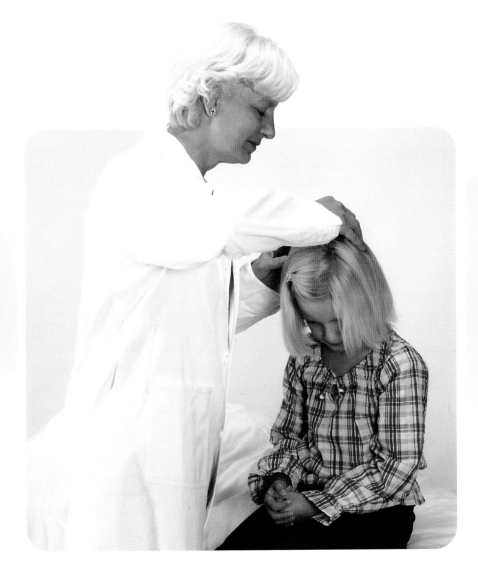

If you think you may have concussion, an adult will take you to hospital or to see a doctor. A nurse or doctor will check whether the injury is serious.

Treating bumps and bruises

Bumps and **bruises** heal themselves. You can help to reduce the **swelling** in a bump by holding an **ice pack** over the **injured** spot.

You need to keep the ice pack in place for
several minutes. You can make an ice pack by
wrapping a packet of frozen peas in a towel.

Getting better

As a **bump** heals, it slowly gets smaller. As a **bruise** heals, it stops hurting and changes colour. It changes from black to purple, green and yellow.

It changes colour as the dead blood is slowly cleared away by fresh blood. Bumps and bruises eventually fade away completely.

Preventing bumps and bruises

Wear protective clothes when you skateboard, or in-line skate. You can wear special pads on your knees and elbows. They will **cushion** you if you fall.

People who play sports wear protective
clothes too. Footballers wear shin pads below
their socks to protect their legs from **bumps**
and **bruises**.

Protect your head

You must take extra care to protect your head. Always wear a **helmet** when you cycle. The helmet **cushions** your head if you have an **accident**.

Falling off a horse can easily **injure** your head. So if you ride a pony, you should always wear a hard hat to protect your head.

Glossary

accident   something that happens by mistake

balance   being able to stand in one position without falling over

baseball   sport like rounders or softball where players hit a ball and run around a series of markers called bases

brain   part of the body that controls the rest of your body. Your brain is inside the top and back of your head.

bruise   blue or black mark on the skin that is caused by a knock

bump   hard lump that forms over a part of the body when it is banged

concussion   when you hit your head very hard and knock your brain

cushion   soften the effect of a knock

flesh   soft muscles and fat that cover your bones

helmet   hard, strong hat that protects your head. It is important to wear a helmet that fits well and is not damaged.

ice pack plastic bag with freezing cold contents used for reducing swelling

injure hurt or damage

injury bump, bruise, cut or break that hurts or damages the body

muscle part of the body that moves the bones or flesh

swelling when part of the body becomes bigger. The swelling is caused by fluid under the skin.

swollen become bigger

unconscious not awake

More books to read

Body Matters: Why Do Bruises Change Colour, And Other Questions About Blood, Angela Royston, (Heinemann Library, 2002)

Safe and Sound: Safety First, Angela Royston, (Heinemann Library, 2001)

No one is allowed to hit and injure you. If anyone hurts you, tell your teacher, nurse or doctor. They will help you. Or you can call Childline in the UK for free on 0800 11 11.

Index

Titles in the *It's Not Catching* series include:

Hardback   0 431 02143 0

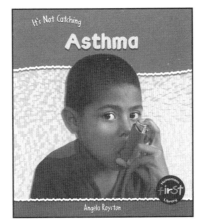

Hardback   0 431 02142 2

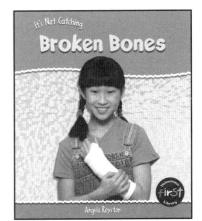

Hardback   0 431 02145 7

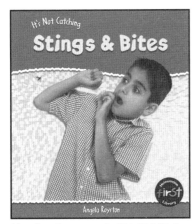

Hardback   0 431 02149 X

Hardback   0 431 02148 1

Hardback   0 431 02144 9

Hardback   0 431 02147 3

Hardback   0 431 02146 5

Find out about the other titles in this series on our website www.heinemann.co.uk/library